AF426282

LARRY THE LOBSTER

Larry the Lobster

Written by Kristin Robinson
as told by Edward D. Harrison III

Illustrated by **Kristen Niedzielski**
Cover Design by *2Faced Design*

Larry the Lobster
Copyright © 2023 by Kristin Robinson

TXu-2-351-460
All rights reserved.

No part of this book may be used or reproduced in any manner
whatsoever, without written permission,
except in the case of brief quotations
embodied in critical articles and reviews.

Illustrations were generated by hand and digital means
on Adobe Illustrator.

First Edition

4

To My Parents:

With Gratitude, I dedicate this book
to my parents, Ed and Dolly, who taught me
to be kind, live a life of integrity,
and to never give up on my dreams.

Once upon a time, a long, long time ago, at the bottom of the ocean, there lived a lobster named Larry. As far as lobsters come, Larry was a good size. Not too big. Not too small. Just right.

6

Larry was a friendly crustacean, although he did his share of chomping!

8

9

One day, Larry was going about his business at the bottom of the ocean floor
when he came upon another lobster twice his size.

Rocky was a crabby guy and began strutting around making shellfish comments, as only lobsters can.

13

Soon enough, a fight began. Even though Larry was quick and mighty,

he was no match for Rocky.

14

When the dirt clouds cleared at the ocean's bottom, Larry was left with only one claw! Oh no! Rocky had chomped it right off!

17

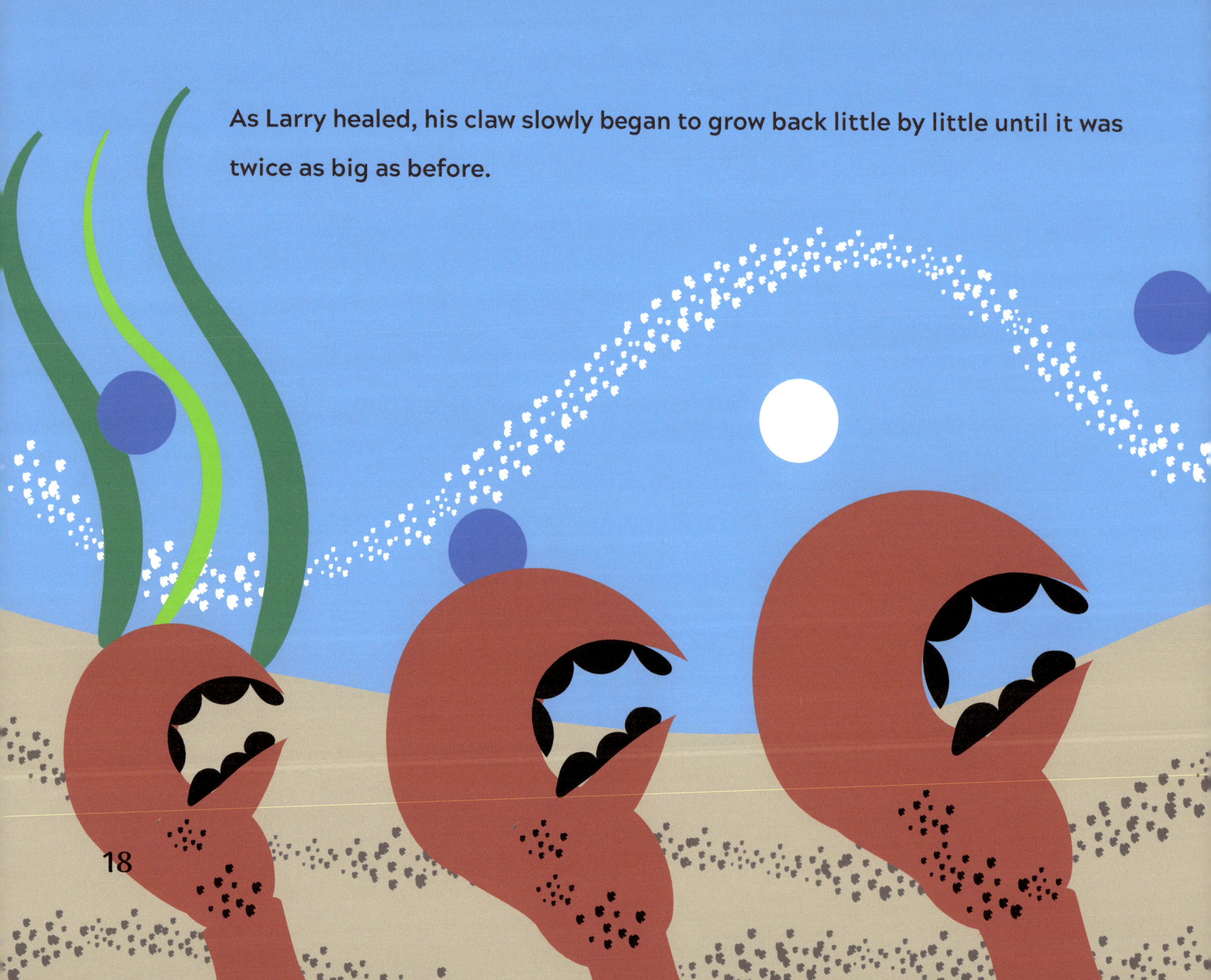

As Larry healed, his claw slowly began to grow back little by little until it was twice as big as before.

Larry was now stronger and mightier than ever! He was so thankful that he proudly walked the ocean floor looking to lend a helpful hand - or claw - to anyone in need.

20

Then one day, Larry came face to face with Rocky, the lobster that had chomped his original claw off. This time the roles were reversed. Larry didn't go around looking for trouble - that wasn't his style. He was a friendly guy with a big heart, and now an even bigger claw! But Larry wouldn't stand for this hard-shelled bully causing any more trouble in these waters.

Larry bravely took one step forward and raised his mighty claw!

Rocky took one look at Larry and slowly backed away. "I don't want any trouble," Rocky said. "With your mighty claw and my massive size, we could team up to help keep everyone safe," he stammered on.

Larry considered this for a moment and then said, "Shore thing!"

The other lobster replied, "Great, but let's NOT shake on it!"

Larry and Rocky smiled as a beautiful new friendship began.

24

The End
25

ABOUT THE AUTHORS

Kristin Robinson, as told by Edward D. Harrison III

Kristin Robinson was born and raised just outside of Boston, Massachusetts. As a child, her Dad would tell this bedtime story to Kristin and her siblings. The story always ended with a few playful lobster chomps from her Dad and an eruption of belly laughs from Kristin and her siblings. It wasn't until later in adulthood that Kristin learned that this story was her Dad's creation. She vowed to get this childhood classic into print. Larry the Lobster is Kristin's first children's book. She currently lives in Arizona with her husband, Mike, and their furry friends, Fenway Frank, Moose, and Tony Biscuits. She is a naturopathic doctor and a graduate of Sonoran University of Health Sciences.

Ed Harrison is a father of four, grandfather of six, and husband to Dolly, his wife of almost 50 years. A lifelong educator, coach, and Athletic Director, Ed currently resides in Massachusetts. Retired in 2016, he continues to support the youth of Wilmington High School by helping with sports camps in the summer and monitoring the halls during the school year. A devoted Boston sports fan, he can be found cheering on his favorite team or lovingly chomping his grandkids in a rendition of this story.

Illustrator:
Kristen M. Niedzielski
Artist from NH
kmncreativityne.com

Cover Design by 2Faced Design

www.ingramcontent.com/pod-product-compliance
Lightning Source LLC
Chambersburg PA
CBHW041033120726

48005CB00004B/795